CITY OF LIGHTS

CITY OF
LIGHTS

LUMINATE
publishing

ISBN 978-0-692-94390-8
Approved for print in Atlanta, Georgia
Printed in the United States of America

All scripture notations, unless otherwise indicated, are taken from the Holy Bible, New International Version®. NIV®.

Details in some anecdotes and stories have been changed at the author's discretion to protect the identities of the persons involved.

978-0-692-94390-8

TABLE OF CONTENTS

01

—

FIRST GIFT

The first gift I ever remember giving in my life was a flower, and I gave it to a stranger.

My family was in a hospital visiting our grandma who was sick with cancer. I was four years old. We had just come from church and I was wearing one of my favorite little Sunday dresses. I'd asked grandma if I could have a flower from her room and she said yes.

After the visit our family walked through a lobby toward the exit, and somewhere along the way I let go of my mom's hand.

On the other side of a large waiting room I had seen a man with his head in his hands, slumped over sitting in a chair against the wall.

I left my family and crossed the room alone past everyone, right to the man.

When I reached him I stopped and waited. He sensed someone standing there and looked up to see me smiling at him. I held up the flower, and he slowly reached out to take it. Then he wept.

I turned around, walked back to my mom, took her hand and kept walking like nothing had happened. She was speechless, having just witnessed something small and sacred.

I don't know what that man in the hospital was going through or who he was. I don't know if he had prayed a prayer that was answered through the flower. But this moment was orchestrated through a four-year-old by a God I know loves him, and in the moment he was given the flower he somehow knew it too.

Experiencing the kindness of God intervene to love someone so simply and perfectly still impacts me. Sometimes I think about the man. Sometimes I worry I heard God more clearly as a four-year-old than I do now.

Years passed, and that childlike giving was replaced with ambition, goals, and the never-ending aim to arrive, whatever that even means. I stopped handing out flowers and started applying for things, reaching for things, and striving for things.

When the whole purpose of life may have been intended to simply hand out little living gifts, I made it more complicated, distracted, and ultimately purposeless.

Over the next two decades I would be without a sense of home as I moved across the country to ten different states for family, education, and career, until a job would eventually take me to Chicago. This is where I would make it, I said. This is where I would arrive.

Little did I know I wouldn't make it in Chicago, at least not in the typical way the world applauds.

Instead I would become more when I became less, go further when I ran slower, and dream more vibrantly when I was less successful. I would find myself when I journeyed back to that original moment of a single flower and the simple act of paying attention.

I now realize the importance of this first gift memory because it was the foreshadowing of what I would need to relearn decades later. I would need to remember the power of a single act for a single person, and the God who delights in orchestrating anything necessary to show us He cares, when our head is in our hands.

02

—

BIG CITY LIGHTS

The day I packed up all my ambition and moved to Chicago was a hot, sticky afternoon in July. The air was thick with humidity and I had never seen so much traffic. Sidewalks seemed as busy as the streets and everyone was in a hurry. A bit overwhelmed by my first big city living experience, I tried not to show it and blend in. I started by pretending that I too was in a hurry.

At that time I saw Chicago only as a footnote in the race to New York City (since Chicago was only the "second city"). Actually the second city reputation had nothing to do with an NYC comparison and more to do with a rebuilding of the city following the Great Fire in 1871, but I didn't know that yet.

There were a lot of things I didn't know yet.

For example, when you live in the big city, carrying groceries home in plastic bags that dig into your hands becomes the worst part of your week. In fact the only thing worse is an apartment without in-unit laundry. Or parking. Without a car I seemed destined to an hour-long CTA train-and-bus-ordeal, and with a car I seemed destined to loop the block endlessly trying to find a parking spot. A parking spot was ironically impossible to spot.

Peaceful coffee shops? Patient traffic guards? Deodorant on the subway? These things don't happen here. I was learning fast.

Aside from the logistical hassles, I was pretty pleased with my new urban lifestyle and impressed by how impressive it was. I couldn't wait for friends to visit and see the epic life I was living in one of the biggest cities in the nation. The skyscrapers, shows, nightlife, and opportunities to learn or be anything you wanted were like a dream.

Then winter came. Not dreaming anymore. Actually, nightmare comes to mind. Let's just say the nickname "Chi-beria" was given for a reason, referencing the similar weather of Siberia. In fact, a news channel reported one day that the temperature in Chicago was colder than the surface of the moon. The *moon*. I remember thinking it equally cruel that we were withstanding these conditions and the meteorologists making that moon comparison.

Instead of focusing on the weather I threw myself deeper into work and social activities. A work-hard-play-hard philosophy was beginning to take over, and in the rare times I was completely honest with myself, I knew I was becoming exhausted, empty, and lonely.

Even in the fierce desolation of winter when both Chicago and I seemed forgotten or rejected by the sun, there were moments of peace. Like when it snowed early in the morning before the chaos began and everything was silent. Silent. Something it never was. I could practically hear the snowflakes settling onto my front porch as I sat and listened to something so still before the world awoke.

A realization was forming that even all the excitement and success this city could offer would not be enough to fill the growing hole inside me, which was beginning to ache and refused to be satisfied.

03

—

GOD OF THIS CITY

Things eventually reached a boiling point at work and in my party life. I saw it all starting to spin out of control but didn't know what to do about it. The same things I used to fill the void felt like they were also creating the void. I was being led further and further down the path of a life I no longer wanted.

Every morning I got up early for work at a corporate marketing job that was slowly draining the life from my eyes, and after work, I stayed out late at bars with friends and colleagues chasing relaxation and escape. Then I'd fall into a restless sleep from exhaustion and do it all over again.

The party life promised fun and fulfillment but only brought me drama and heartbreak. I was being continually promoted at work, and on the fast track to becoming an executive. It wasn't long before senior leadership tapped me on the shoulder to manage a multi-million dollar private label business. It was an amazing and rare opportunity for someone of my age and limited experience.

The moment I 'arrived' was one I'll never forget. I was on the top floor of the Executive Wing, a part of the building I had once seen as unreachable. While presenting to a packed boardroom of executive leadership with the Chicago skyline staring back at me through the windows, I remember thinking how completely passionless I felt. I had made it, but I was miserable.

It wasn't until I made it to the top of the Summit that I realized I hated the Mountain.

Recognition, exposure, and money; I began to see this trap for what it was. Never-ending, and never enough. I then arrived at the discouraging and overdue conclusion that I would never have a meaningful life with these meaningless goals.

"Whoever loves money never has enough;
whoever loves wealth is never satisfied with their income.
This too is meaningless."
Ecclesiastes 5:10

To make my internal struggle even worse, God seemed to be following me around these days. Everywhere I went. And I clearly sensed He wasn't just there to comfort me. He was there to get my attention.

By now the growing emptiness inside had become closer to depression. While complaining about my problems to several people later that week, someone asked me if I was 'saved.' My immediate reaction was to be offended by the question. God already made sense to me so the requirement that I specifically needed Jesus to be saved and go to heaven felt unnecessary, judgmental, and religious.

But not for long. Just days later as I was walking home alone through the city, the saved conversation came to mind again.

This time it was nagging at the hole inside me and wouldn't go away. Finally out of discouragement and basically desperation, I just spoke to that "somewhere out there" and told Jesus I didn't fully understand Him or this, but accepted that He was God and Savior like He said. That I'd have Him if He'd have me.

Then I understood why people called it saved. Relief washed over me in every way and it was like the weight of a thousand pounds was lifted. I no longer felt insecure, alone, or unsure of where I stood with God. Somehow a peace now covered all those things.

I realize my 'prayer' wasn't the more eloquent, scripted versions I've heard spoken in churches since then, but it worked. Or at least it must have. Because whatever happened in that moment was real and I've never been the same since. The hole inside was miraculously, instantly filled up with light. And it felt like a miracle.

Things changed after that, a lot.

The changes were gradual but big. The way I saw myself, prioritized things, and invested my time were all eventually affected. I stopped wasting my after-work hours at bars and started filling my schedule with places and people who could care about me. It was intimidating to get involved in a church without knowing anyone. But I had undeniably just had some type of Jesus-experience and figured, they of all people, would understand.

Around this time the Chris Tomlin version of the song "God of this City" was everywhere. When I listened to the lyrics something new stirred in me for the city.

> *"You're the God of this city*
> *You're the King of these people*
> *You're the Lord of this nation*
> *You're the Light in this darkness*
> *You're the Hope to the hopeless*
> *You're the Peace to the restless*
> *There is no one like our God*
> *For greater things have yet to come*
> *And greater things are still to be done in this city"*

I was beginning to see a different city. One that Jesus cared about and one that I should care about. Not just because it was fun or exciting but because of its people.

While my priorities and desires were shifting, it felt uncomfortable and beyond my control. Sometimes I tried to fight against it and go back to the old way of living, but now that felt so awful I couldn't bear it. I eventually began to see there was only one way forward and that was God's way.

That August on a hot summer morning, I was baptized in Lake Michigan alongside friends and the support of a small crowd. This public act of commitment and obedience brought a rush of release and seemed to seal a new life. I left my regrets and wounds in the water as I stepped back onto the beach with full freedom and a fresh start. My heart felt purified and the burden completely gone. I would no longer have to be perfect but just have faith in Jesus who is.

Now I had truly become a part of the Big City Lights. I was a Light in the City.

04

—

A BETTER DREAM

Turns out God's next priority to address was my ever-so-sacred career. Soon after I accepted an offer for a bigger opportunity and quit my current job, the offer fell through. I then found myself unemployed for what I thought could be a few weeks but would become six months.

Without income there weren't many places I could afford to live in the city anymore. It felt like I went from top to bottom overnight. With no job prospects in sight or any interviews, I planned to live off my savings account as long as I could. Also around this time the romantic relationship I was in had ended. So far from my limited perspective, it would seem that accepting Jesus had definitely made my life worse, not better.

I was confused. New in faith, I prayed for direction or answers. Or something. I waited and listened and sometimes was filled with faith and trust, and other times wasn't so loyal.

Rock bottom happened the night a friend and I had dinner. I didn't have the money to eat at a restaurant so I had suggested she come to my place. I also didn't have much food in the apartment, so I heated up a couple cans of soup and paired it with saltines. Then completely to my surprise the moment we sat down at the table, I started to cry. Deep cry. Grief had apparently decided it had been locked up for too long, and now wasn't leaving until it had been sufficiently heard.

So there I sat crying in my soup. I barely noticed my friend trying to console me as I dripped into minestrone. After a long and aimless six months I didn't have hope or energy left, and considering I had spent most of my life being successful, I was also ashamed.

No longer on top of the world anymore, I was ready to humble myself to a new level. And I would later find out that in God's economy that's exactly when things start to turn around for the better.

The next morning brought a grief hangover and I was tired from the tears of the night before. I needed to get out of this apartment.

I wandered purposeless to the end of the city and beginning of the coastline, and sat in the sand at North Avenue beach. Staring blankly at the dark blue line that separated the cloudy sky and Lake Michigan, the discouraging thoughts crept in: *Why was this happening to me? What am I supposed to do now?*

The first question wouldn't be answered for me until years later, but the second was answered almost instantly:

A thin, clear thought came to mind. It was like a thousand other thoughts were cleared out in a moment and just one dropped in. The thought was pure and not mine. *If I wanted a job I could create one.*

Through the authority of that brief moment, I had the distinct impression God wanted me to create a marketing company to spread *His* messages in the world.

The warning that accompanied this revelation was that it would be His work, His way; not mine. And for His reputation; not mine. Basically I sat there realizing I had just been given a job offer from the Author of the Universe, aka Best Boss Ever.

I accepted the opportunity and the terms.

Now I had a new dream, which admittedly was much better than any of the ones I had tried to create on my own. I had a purpose. And I had work to do.

05

—

BABY BIRD

What began as a whisper grew in the weeks and months that followed into a passion for starting a company called Luminate Marketing, with a purpose to illuminate the messages of Christ in the world.

It felt like I was walking all over the city with a secret friend, and I say secret because no one else saw it.

News of my brand new employment opportunity had mixed reviews. Some were thrilled and shared my relief. Others looked concerned, saying nonprofits were called that for a reason. My parents started calling more often just to 'check in' and friends started offering to buy my lunch.

At the time it appeared to be a perfect storm because a recession had just hit that was the worst since the 1930s. But even then, I suspected this timing may have been divinely chosen so that one day I could look back, and know only God could be responsible for a victory. He would get the glory for pulling off something so seemingly impossible.

Jesus looked at them and said,
"With man this is impossible,
but with God all things are possible."
Matthew 19:26

I had to hold on with white knuckles to what God had given because everywhere I went it seemed like people were trying to take it away from me. Friends and family had an uncomfortable amount of questions about my ability to make a living serving only churches and nonprofits.

Looking back I now know God's ways are the opposite of the world's ways so of course everyone wouldn't understand. And His plans are big so they are usually scary. In fact, if this vision had the full support of everyone and wasn't much of a stretch for me to accomplish, I may have reconsidered where it really came from.

I've learned that when God stirs in our hearts to do something for Him, it can require a fight. We may need to protect, and hide, and feed the vision like a baby bird before it can fly in plain sight. Because the early days are the most vulnerable and God, not the world, should be given access to see it, shape it, and speak life into it.

So I stopped talking about it and started praying about it. I stopped dreaming for it and started working for it.

"Come," he said. Then Peter got down out of the boat,
walked on the water and came toward Jesus.
But when he saw the wind, he was afraid and,
beginning to sink, cried out, "Lord, save me!"
Immediately Jesus reached out his hand and caught him.
"You of little faith," he said, "why did you doubt?"
Matthew 14:29-31

When I looked around at my circumstances and resources I panicked and doubted, but when I looked at God I trusted. For a while I had to avoid the skepticism of others so I wouldn't lose focus and faith.

I decided to protect, and feed, and love the baby bird. This would work. Because God gave it to me, the world needs this, and I need this.

06

—

LAUNCH

Without references, work portfolios, a website or even business cards, I wasn't much of a marketing company. All I had was an idea, but was also familiar with the quote that said, "Nothing is more powerful than an idea whose time has come."

Completely against what I had learned in business school and the counsel of seasoned professionals, I created a simple business model called: "Work For Free." Because the company served churches and nonprofits, people frequently asked if Luminate itself was a nonprofit. I used to respond with a grin that yes, it was a nonprofit, if by that you mean not profitable.

It worked. The perfect launch strategy turned out to be giving my time and work away for free. Apparently churches and nonprofits hate to turn down free services.

This approach didn't earn me a dollar but gained the references, credibility, and exposure I needed. Google and the Holy Spirit (not in that order) were also helping me absorb new information needed for this God-appointed role at an incredible rate. In fact in meetings with my 'clients' I started saying things – wise things – and honestly had no idea where they were coming from. I was saying things I hadn't learned before. I had solutions to problems they hadn't even told me they had yet.

I considered these instances to be heavenly nods and confirmation to keep pressing forward when I felt alone or didn't see progress.

When I had reached five solid case studies I built the Luminate website around them, focusing on the work, results, and testimonials. Soon I had my very first client (not the free kind!) and it felt like such a milestone of God's provision and faithfulness that I took a picture of the first check for $300. I even thought about just saving the check and not cashing it for sentimental reasons, but needed the money so, a picture would do.

I celebrated by getting a second client. And then a third. Now that there were clients this company could grow momentum soon and needed an official launch.

Invitations for a 'black tie affair' went out to friends, family, clients, advocates, and anyone who hadn't laughed when I told them my new career path. Actually I invited them too. Then I used the $300 for flowers, food, a logo cake, and gifts for the guests. A good friend who would later become one of our videographers, created a motion graphics launch video for the event. I was ready.

When the evening came it was exhilarating. Guests arrived dressed in their best, which definitely contributed to the legitimacy and professionalism of the launch. After everyone had arrived I passed out bright glow sticks (the color of the Luminate logo of course), and then abruptly shut off all the lights. It was completely dark.

In the darkness the launch video began to play on a big screen. While people watched the video I looked around the room at all the glow sticks; every light a support and encouragement. Every light a reminder that what God had promised was coming true.

The video was flawless and afterwards guests clapped and cheered. I didn't want the lights to come back on so I could keep this moment, and also so I could keep private the happy tears flooding my face.

It didn't matter that I had little experience and no employees. It didn't matter that this was the worst economic recession in eighty years. It didn't matter that churches and nonprofits aren't profitable. All that mattered in this moment was that God wanted this to happen and it was happening.

07

—

IN THE MIDDLE

Growing a startup from scratch brought with it the reality of sacrifice.

It began with somewhat nominal sacrifices like cheap food, discount clothing, and walking instead of taking the train. But eventually there became a threat of more personal sacrifices like losing the apartment I had loved and built a home in. The stable oasis of this place was by far the most valuable thing I had in the city.

The apartment sacrifice being an absolute last resort, I sold my car. When that wasn't enough I decided to sell everything I could part with on Craigslist. This essentially included all furniture, artwork, and anything else I suspected could possibly be trendy or purchase-worthy.

On the day I sat in my lovely home watching people walk away with my treasures, my faith was tested. Again. This company barely existed, and I was sure making a lot of sacrifices on its behalf.

When even this approach didn't generate enough income for rent, a friend from church offered me a spare room at her place and I gladly took it. Goodbye, apartment.

Interestingly enough losing my home would actually prepare me for what was next.

God began nudging my heart to see things I wouldn't normally notice. One afternoon while shopping for office supplies downtown, a person lying against the side of a building caught my eye. And I didn't just notice him, I *saw* him. I couldn't look away. It was clear he had probably slept there, in that spot, all night.

I knew it wasn't just my own financial pressure creating compassion. A work of God was allowing me to see people in a new way for the first time.

A few days later, a girl on the train caught my eye. Months ago I would have assumed this affluent young professional had it all together, but what I saw now reminded me of the burden I used to carry. Especially on the train, a place where I spent lot of my time, I began sensing the burdens of fellow passengers.

Soon I couldn't walk by the shiny skyscrapers and not see the alleys. I couldn't be thinking and texting, without somehow glancing over just in time to see someone climb down from a city dumpster looking for something to eat.

How is it possible I had lived here so long without noticing *this* city? I hadn't been looking, and definitely hadn't been seeing. And once I saw I felt accountable.

In the middle of all the exciting attractions this place had to offer, there were people. People who had been there all along. In the middle of my day, in the middle of my errands, in the middle of the space between buildings, in the middle of two blankets, in the middle of despair.

And somehow in the middle of my shiny city life I started seeing a lot less glitter and a lot more sorrow.

08

—

NOT MY BIRTHDAY

I became more involved in church and ended up meeting a tall, dark and handsome (no, seriously) man that would later become my husband. The church had an outreach ministry we served in together to learn more about homelessness, and grow our shared awareness of people in the middle.

But it wasn't until after we were married and moved into an apartment along the Chicago River that we entered into homelessness in an unexpected way.

I remember the day it happened because it was my birthday.

That year I still wanted to plan something special but not by choosing from the usual list of options. The more I had been sensing the burdens of others, the more I wanted to see them lifted as they had been for me.

A day guaranteed to be 'all about me' didn't sound as appealing as it used to. I considered the potential party, fancy dinner, and gifts. I thought of the money that would be spent. And I was having a hard time getting excited about the traditional annual itinerary.

Instead of expecting the spotlight this year I'd be happy to be a light for someone else, but didn't know how or for who.

Of course in God's perfect timing, later that week, I was telling a friend about this birthday wish and she told me there was a guy that slept down by the river in a tent.

A *tent?* Out in the cold, during January, in this Chicago winter? I couldn't believe it.

Turns out it wasn't just him. There were over thirty tents along the river, filled with people who won't or can't get into shelters for the winter.

I knew God had placed the hope of giving in my heart this year for them.

It got even more unbelievable from there. I would soon find out the tents were in our backyard. Literally. The South Loop building we lived in was along the river, and this community was camped out over a hill I could see from our window. But the hill hid the tents from being seen, so we had lived there for a year and never even knew they were there.

But now we knew. And we were accountable for the knowledge that our *neighbors* were sleeping outside.

It was so bitterly cold that week as we gathered coats, blankets, and warm clothing. I thought of our newfound neighbors constantly, especially when I was outside, and wondered how they were surviving these frigid conditions.

The day of my birthday was spent preparing for the tents visit the following morning. When the day came and went without a celebration, it was honestly a little disappointing. I was happy without the party, but ended up not getting a birthday song either. This was the first birthday of my life without the song and I was surprised how that felt like a loss somehow.

The next morning I woke up early to put several homemade breakfast casseroles in the oven. As the food baked I sat in the stillness of our home, cuddled up with a blanket and cup of hot tea. I watched the sun slowly rise over that hillside by the river. I wondered what God had planned this morning and who we would meet.

When it was time to go, I unexpectedly felt a little nervous. My husband and I gathered everything and met half a dozen friends to walk over to the tents together.

When we arrived I was completely intimidated, out of my comfort zone, and silenced by poverty. The tent city was silent in the cold morning air and was covered in trash, old clothing, and rat traps. The thought crossed my mind that this may have been a mistake. I had no idea how many people were actually living in all of these tents or who they were. As my eyes scanned the broken bikes, worn out shoes, and general debris of the area I couldn't believe I was standing in my country, in my city, and in my backyard.

At first, people just stayed in their tents. I assume they were thinking the same thing I was: *who are these people.* Until now I didn't even consider the fact that they wouldn't know who *we* were or even why we were there. And it's possible this community didn't receive many positive visitors.

We started walking through the community, calling out, "Good morning! Hot breakfast and coffee for you!"

After a few minutes, several tents started rustling inside, and I hoped that meant they were coming out to meet us. They were. Timid at first, several people came out and accepted a cup of hot coffee. Once the breakfast casseroles were opened and the smell of hot, homemade food drifted through the community, more people appeared. The sound of conversation slowly began and then eventually some laughter.

As breakfast was served we also walked around and met each person individually, asking their names and telling them ours. The blankets, coats, hats, gloves, and toiletry items were appreciated, but the McDonald's gift cards were a huge hit. On a note attached with each card we had written, *"You are loved and worthy of love."*

Conversation about what people needed was a good icebreaker and we took mental notes for a future visit. Eventually we were asked why we were there. We said because we want you to know that *Jesus is watching out for you and so are we.*

After a few cups of coffee and enough food to go around, it started to feel like an outdoor living room. Once we all let our guards down and became more comfortable together it was surprisingly fun.

There were clearly some informal comedians in the group, and the more people showed up, the more fun we had. When the food was finished, some still stuck around for another hour or so to 'help us polish off the coffee.'

A friend announced it was my birthday and the singing started.

The birthday song.

Tears came to my eyes when I realized that this moment, by the river with new friends, was the gift God wanted to give me this year.

A song to show me how beautiful it is to serve when I'm supposed to be served, to give when I'm supposed to be given, and the peace that comes from knowing: it's not all about me.

09

—

A NEW NORMAL

What we didn't know then was that this harmless little birthday party would change our lives.

Now that we had met the tent community and knew what they looked like, we started seeing them everywhere. And they started seeing us. We'd spot each other on the red line, along State or Roosevelt, or on the sidewalk outside the 711. Sometimes on our way to work, church, or the grocery store we'd wave or maybe stop and talk for a while. In this crazy, hectic city full of millions of people we were becoming *neighbors*.

I would never have guessed that people I just met would so soon be in my neighborhood, in my life, and somehow even in my heart. I started thinking about them while I was in meetings at work, or wonder how they were doing when there was a thunderstorm. I found myself wanting to know more about their stories, job situations, and family lives.

They were fascinating people; so resourceful and resilient. Some had cell phones, or dogs as pets, or a campsite setup more impressive than an award-winning KOA. Others were funny or shy, gruff or kind, and some wanted to get to know us. Some looked too young to be homeless and some too old to be homeless. Others were young but already seemed old.

One of the easiest things to connect on was how horrible the weather was, probably a topic that has been bringing Chicagoans together since the dawn of time. Another crowd favorite was how annoying public transit is (specifically the bus system), and why the people on tour boats floating down the river didn't return the gesture when we waved hello. We talked about the ducks that kept waddling out of the river and up onto the bank expecting a snack from us. We talked about the severe rat problem in the tent city.

These people I had gone to serve on my birthday were becoming my friends. Big difference.

People used to ask us what church or humanitarian organization we were with. That doesn't happen much anymore, and I'm glad. There's no longer a clear line of serving and being served. And the good thing about a Chicago winter is you can't tell who's homeless because we're all bundled up in the same five layers of clothing.

I could feel myself changing. I was starting to become loyal to these people, and when I rode the CTA to work and heard comments about 'bums' sleeping on the train, or areas of downtown that weren't nice anymore because of 'beggars,' it bothered me. People that would purposefully ignore someone trying to talk to them from a seat on the sidewalk, bothered me.

A lot more things than normal were starting to bother me.

10

—

THE SIGN

My new friends were quick to educate me when I said something naïve, close-minded, or incorrect. Turns out I knew next to nothing about homelessness.

An early lesson learned was that it's not always hard to become homeless. The way it was described to me is that when there isn't much if any family to begin with, the path to being without support or options can be a fairly short one. Made sense.

I thought back to when I started Luminate, having been given opportunities for education and relationships. Without those things my story too could have included a shelter, because a limited network creates limited opportunities.

I learned one of the most valuable things an education or job provides is a network; access to other people to earn credibility with and rely on for future opportunities. Access I'd always taken for granted.

Another thing I learned was that not everyone had burned bridges in their lives to end up without options. Sometimes it was the opposite. They may have been the ones depending on a spouse who left, or on the receiving side of abuse. But of course not every story played out that way either.

Some were even simpler than that: life was just hard. One bad situation too many, had turned into a few nights in a shelter, had turned into hopelessness, which had turned into a lifestyle. And it was hard to know how or if to ever climb back out again after that.

Before I actually knew any homeless people I had mostly thought of them as sitting on the sidewalk with a cup for coins. Or holding a cardboard sign. Honestly I used to think this was a business model for them, or an arrangement so they wouldn't have to work, or a way to pay for drugs and alcohol, or just something they didn't really mind doing during the day.

And then on a jog through the city after work one evening, my husband and I saw a friend of ours sitting along the sidewalk. At first I just saw her and her backpack – but then I saw the sign.

We paused our run to stop and say hello. As we talked, I started noticing people walking by and looking at us. Maybe they were wondering why we were standing with a homeless person. Maybe they thought we were trying to be the hero. I have no idea. One thing I do know is that I had never stopped and talked with a homeless person in public before – not while they were holding the sign.

There was something shameful about the sign. Something powerless. And the longer we stood there, the more I became aware of it. The sign and the shame. I quickly glanced around to see all the well-dressed young professionals walking home from work, who would catch my eye and then look away, and a bit of the sign shame began to become mine. It felt like I was wearing the sign just by standing there.

I used to think of the homeless as 'homeless people.' But it makes a difference when I think of them as people, not homeless people.

They just don't have a street address but aren't a different type of person.

Anyone can end up without a place to call home, and most of us have probably felt lost or without roots at some point in our lives, even if not sleeping outside. Until I think of the homeless as just like anyone else I can't picture my sibling or spouse in that situation. Because I don't feel my friends or family deserve to live that way. But no one deserves it.

Now I think of homelessness as a challenging life circumstance to be overcome. And we all have those.

Jesus said, "the Son of Man has no place to lay His head" (Luke 9:58). Even God didn't have a place to call home while on earth. But He was no less valuable or less impactful or less in any way. He was still who He was. Just no address.

I liked these people. And I liked how we enjoyed spending time together. Although I'd soon find out as I got more involved, that it wouldn't stay this simple. Because their lives weren't this simple.

Later I had asked my friend with the sign how often she 'does that' (I didn't know what else to call it) and if it bothers her. She began talking about the sign, emotionless, as if telling me how often she visits the public library.

"Oh, about every other day or so."

I nodded and left a pause for her to continue if she wanted to.

She explained why she had no other option but the sign, and then her eyes filled with tears as she said how ashamed she was to have to beg.

The sign is an injustice because it is a lack of dignity. It's a white flag made of cardboard signaling surrender and defeat. And after I learned the truth about the sign, I never wanted anyone to have to hold it ever again.

11

—

OPEN HEART
OPEN HOME

I was learning to love people without homes but was also about to learn what that love would require.

We were having breakfast down by the tents along the river one Saturday morning, and there was a new guy. No one knew much about him, which was rare at the tents.

He was young and probably no more than thirty but looked old. He seemed nervous and paranoid, constantly looking over his shoulder. The first thing I noticed about him was how jittery he was; almost physically shaking. Even from my limited experience with street life so far, I could see he had the common symptoms of a heroin addict.

He said he lived further down the river and had heard about us serving breakfast. He wanted us to understand he was only here for the breakfast. Fair enough.

But then he was very eager to receive anything and everything we had to offer. I quickly gathered he was in worse circumstances than everyone else. When he was passed some hand warmers, I saw him immediately shove them into his pockets, as if to conceal something valuable. He was also clearly hungry.

I wanted to learn more about him and how we could connect him with resources. To my surprise I asked if we could come visit him where he lived, and also to my surprise, he said yes.

He lived on the other side of the bridge further away from everyone else along the river. But when we arrived we saw he didn't even have a tent. For the past few months he'd been barely surviving subzero temperatures with a real threat of literally freezing. To keep out of the wind, he had created an area against the side of a river trench, and was using cardboard and trash to stay warm at night.

This is something you can't un-see.

The Bible says to *"Carry each other's burdens, and in this way you will fulfill the law of Christ" (Galatians 6:2)*, and when I saw the miserable life he was living, I wanted to enter into it and share his burden.

We invited him to come out to lunch with us, which turned into an afternoon of errands to get him some much-needed essentials. When it was late afternoon and time for us to head home, I couldn't bear sending him back to the cold trench. We asked him to come over to our place for dinner.

We'd never had a homeless person in our home before.

That night while dinner was cooking I offered to do his laundry. But when I pulled the clothes out of his bag to wash them, the smell was so overwhelming that it triggered a gag reflex, and I gagged. I didn't want him to see my reaction so I looked away, closed my eyes, and took a moment to gather myself.

I looked around and worried we'd have to throw everything we owned made of fabric away, because the smell was so thick it was filling up the house. And he was sitting on our couch.

This was one of the first major tests of my old life versus new life. Spending time with people without homes felt different than *my* home being affected. It was time to decide which was more important, our stuff or our friends.

I tried to push out materialism and the 'this is too far' thought rising in my mind, so God's love could rush in and cover it all. And I asked for forgiveness. And I asked for the strength to be more like Him and less like me.

"For we brought nothing into the world,
and we can take nothing out of it.
But if we have food and clothing,
we will be content with that."
1 Timothy 6:7-8

Then he said to them, "Watch out!
Be on your guard
against all kinds of greed;
life does not consist in an abundance of possessions."
Luke 12: 15

This hesitation to love exposed an idol of materialism and greed in me. And I hated it.

So I rejected my thoughts, did the laundry, and considered throwing the couch out far better than letting a parasite grow in my heart that wouldn't host a stranger.

After dinner we played Scrabble. I was starting to stall in sending him back 'home' again.

My husband and I had already discussed boundaries, and one of them was that we must know someone well before they spent the night. They also needed to be free of drug addictions, which could invite unpredictable or dangerous scenarios. I knew this was a safety measure for our family and what we had agreed to. I also knew neither qualification was met through this young man, but my heart still wanted warmth and rest for him.

When he went to the bathroom my husband and I discussed privately. Later we tried to casually bring up the topic of conversation that he could stay with us if he wanted to.

He didn't want to.

He wanted to go back to his spot that night along the river so someone else didn't take it. I was surprised, disappointed, and relieved all at once.

He did ask if he could shower before heading back.

While he showered, I folded his laundry, and in the silence let my mind wander to how serving and giving are not the same.

Serving is what I had been doing for years. But now I was learning to *give*. To give my time, my convenience, my home, and my heart. I was opening myself up to care, to be hurt, and to be disappointed. Because that's what you do when you love-for-real. Ironically, serving always sounded more noble to me than giving, but giving is what cost me more. It was also one of the most fulfilling things I had ever experienced.

I have learned that helping someone carry their burdens requires much more than serving breakfast by the river on a Saturday morning. It means opening up your heart and maybe even your home.

12

—

GETTING INTO THE TRENCHES

People were concerned for our safety when we started letting the homeless into our home. But we were suspicious that safety could just be fear disguised as wisdom, and saw it as another potential idol to avoid. Our safety or sense of home didn't seem more valuable than another person's safety or sense of home. And sometimes our home *was* their safety, even if just for a shower or a meal.

One evening after dinner, our new friend living along the river confided in us that he had recently been released from prison, after a seven-year sentence. That explained why no one at the tents knew who he was. He didn't say what the sentence was for but only that it was a felony charge. I nodded, but in my mind started thinking through all possible escape routes from our apartment.

I needed to reject the thoughts in my mind again. This time I replaced fear with the reminder to rest in the peace and protection of Christ, and to just *listen* to him.

He explained that when released he had nowhere to go, and with a felony charge was unable to find work. To this day I don't know what he was in prison for, because I never asked and because it didn't matter. What mattered was getting him out of the trench, out of the cold, and into a life where he could actually start living again.

We learned he had been surviving by finding public garages to stay warm in for a few hours each night. He didn't want to get caught, so he had forced himself to stay awake during those hours. After months of this routine he was of course exhausted. I remember the first time he came to church with us and fell asleep, and rather than being annoyed I was completely relieved.

I had an idea. I knew some of the tents had propane heaters that people used to survive through the winter. At least as a short-term solution we needed to get him one, and fast.

The night we went to the river to take him a heater was one I'll never forget.

I have never been so cold in my life. Something was extra cutting that night about the wind whipping off the river, and I had to turn my face away to avoid windburn or frostbite. I had never experienced an icy wind so sharp and painful. Maybe it's always this miserable down by the Chicago River late at night in February. I guess I wouldn't really know.

We couldn't get the heater to work. I waited while my husband and friend worked together trying to fix it. My eyes watered from the unforgiving winter, and from my desperation for God to reach down and save this man from these unbearable circumstances. It broke my heart to think of him reduced to sleeping out here for months.

Once the heater started working we all huddled together next to it to get warm, and I looked up into the dark.

"Remember those who are in prison,
as though you were in prison with them.
Remember those who are suffering,
as though you were suffering as they are."
Hebrews 13:3 (GNT)

We suffered with him that night.

And we comforted him, saying he wouldn't be living this way for long and that we both saw something special in him. That he wasn't a 'homeless person.' When we treat a person like they are loved and worthy of love they start to act like it. And eventually they start to believe it.

He wasn't the same discouraged person after that, and I believe it was from the warmth of the heater and the words God gave us to speak to him that night.

I'm glad I learned to cry out to Jesus in desperation on behalf of someone else. And I'm glad it was for him.

Getting 'into the trenches' with someone isn't just a phrase for me anymore. I know it's literal now. Sometimes it requires literally getting into the trenches by the river with someone on a cold and miserable night, just so they don't have to be alone.

13

—

NOW OR NEVER

I was leaving church one Sunday morning and felt someone pull at my arm. It was our friend and he looked awful. He had a black eye, and was sick and shaking. There was a new desperation in his eyes and I wondered if he had been without drugs for a while.

He hadn't been on drugs but was suicidal.

He'd shown up at church that morning hoping to find us, but hadn't expected a perfectly timed sermon about the trap of addiction. He described what he said felt like God speaking just to him during the service, and it was clear he was having a spiritual breakthrough. He said he knew he needed help and didn't want to live this way anymore. Jesus was trying to get his attention. I knew because I recognized my own turning point on his face.

We all knew he couldn't move forward in life with this addiction because it would continue to suffocate his progress until it was addressed. We all knew God wanted to heal his heart more than his homelessness. And we were ready to say *yes* to whatever role we were asked to play, but didn't know what that was.

Of course we already had previous commitments; I had made coffee plans followed by a promised double date, to take another couple out to lunch and celebrate a new job. But I felt God wanted us to help him right now and that it couldn't wait.

So we canceled everything.

A close friend and former addict had previously told us about a great Christian drug and alcohol addiction rehabilitation program. He said it had transformed his life, and as we were standing there outside the church not sure what to do, *he actually walked by*. Obviously not a coincidence.

We told him the situation and asked what to do. He explained it was extremely uncommon to get a person into the program in less than two weeks, due to the forms and background check requirements. But, this moment might not come again. If possible we had to act while God still had his attention and before heroin took it away again.

Through this friend of ours making phone calls in the moment from the sidewalk, an on-the-spot phone interview with the Director, and absolutely remarkable favor, we were able to 'bypass the system.'

But they said we had to bring him in right away before intake was closed for the day.

There was tight security at the facility, and we were screened at the door. The door closed behind us with a sound that was loud and institutional, like what I would have imagined for a jail. I wasn't sure I wanted to leave him here. We were led down a hallway to an intake room, and the staff left us to get paperwork. As soon as we were alone, our friend started to sob in surrender and despair, and our hearts grieved with his.

Soon a staff person entered the room and abruptly requested he empty his pockets. As I watched him remove the lighters, knives, and other items to put them on the table in front of us, the cold night by the river came to mind. It felt similar to this somehow. It was that same familiar feeling of getting into the trenches with someone to enter into their circumstances and share in their grief. And it was heavy.

We never know where we'll end up when we listen to God.

I didn't think I'd be sitting in a drug and alcohol rehabilitation center when I got dressed for church that morning, but there was nowhere else I'd rather be.

My husband and I filled out the paperwork and put our signatures down as his sponsors for the length of the program. They explained we would be able to talk with him by phone after two weeks and see him after a month. The intake team left us alone for a few minutes, before he would be taken into the program for fourteen months.

This was a big commitment we were all making.

We prayed out loud together knowing we wouldn't see each other for a while. We were in agreement that this was hard, but good.

Today had brought a rare breakthrough and it felt like everything else planned had needed to wait.

Because sometimes an opportunity is just that; and it's now or never.

14

—

AMAZING MERCY

Mercy is like a life preserver. Sometimes we need it, but aren't willing to accept it until we've been so beaten down by the raging river of life, that we have no choice but to accept it before the next set of rapids comes. Mercy is the life preserver that relieves our suffering long enough for us to catch our breath. It's the kindness of God, but also the cancellation of our mistakes. And that's what Jesus is all about.

I imagine living on the streets sometimes, and wonder how it would change me. I wonder what I would need the most. Maybe more than money or a job, I'd need mercy. To be looked in the eye or receive a caring touch on the shoulder, or a smile that was genuine, or for someone to ask my name. I imagine it's possible these simple acts of mercy could impact how I felt about my circumstances, my day, my hope for the future, or even myself.

The definition of mercy is *"compassion or forgiveness shown toward someone whom it is within one's power to punish or harm. It is performed out of a desire to relieve suffering that is motivated by compassion."*

Mercy seems similar to grace. But the definition of grace is *"the free and unmerited favor of God, as manifested in the salvation of sinners and the bestowal of blessings. Or courteous goodwill."*

I've heard a lot about grace but seemingly little about mercy. "Extend grace to others" or "extend grace to yourself" or "grace changes everything" are common phrases. There's even a song called *Amazing Grace* (and a movie, etc).

But there is just something so powerful to me about the word *mercy*. It seems extravagant and unexpected. It seems dramatic and epic. It seems like life and death hang in the balance.

Recently, out of curiosity, I wrote out the lyrics of *Amazing Grace* with the word *mercy* inserted.

Amazing mercy
how sweet the sound
That saved a wretch like me.
I once was lost but now I'm found.
Was blind but now I see.
'Twas mercy that taught
my heart to fear
And mercy my fears relieved.
How precious did
that mercy appear
The hour I first believed.
Through many dangers,
toils and snares,
I have already come;
'Tis mercy hath brought
me safe thus far,
And mercy will lead me home.
Amazing mercy,
how sweet the sound
That saved a wretch like me.

I once was lost, but now I'm found.
Was blind, but now I see.

Or, the quote below puts it more simply.

Grace is God giving us what we don't deserve, and mercy is God not giving us what we do deserve.

It's mercy that catches my attention when I'm walking down the street and notice someone else's needs. It's mercy that allows me to hold someone smelly or dirty in my arms because they need comfort more than I need control. It's mercy that welcomes people who deserve judgment to be spared in compassion.

Mercy is amazing. And if mercy really is a life preserver, we should all spend our lives passing out as many flotation devices as possible.

Since Jesus has demonstrated the ultimate act of mercy, I can't think of a better way to spend my limited time on earth, than sharing the fantastic news of who He is and what He's done.

He has passed us all a life preserver and all we have to do is take it.

15
—

THE JOURNEY CONTINUES

Some days are still normal around here. I wake up, walk the puppy, go to work, come home and make dinner, and enjoy an evening with family. Ordinary stuff.

Other days I'm texted from the tents with emergency needs while I'm in a meeting. Or there is a disagreement at the tents and I'm called, then texted, then called, and then texted again.

Some days I'm asked to be a mediator, a psychologist, or just to make a few tacos. And I never know which days will be which. They are all starting to run together.

This new life is overlapping and crazy and beautiful and running together. Interruptions have become so normalized, that in a weird way, they feel somewhat comforting.

However, not every day brings a victory. Some days are hard, frustrating, uncomfortable, and inconvenient. Some days I'm pushed to my limits and see the worst of myself ('scary self') come out. But overall it's real, and hard, and satisfying. Sometimes all at once.

So basically, it's love.

The more I learn about love the less I realize I know about it. Loving people who love me back isn't the same experience as giving to people who need so much, take so much, and often give nothing in return. Unconditional love is a wild rollercoaster that sometimes involves free-falls or an upside-down pit in the stomach.

It's intriguing to watch how God works. He leads, one step at a time, and as our trust grows our faith grows. He asks us to do something that seems big, and we say yes. Then he asks us to do something that's bigger, and we say yes. And pretty soon we are saying yes to things that would have seemed absolutely crazy a few months ago. How wise and gentle God is to grow us over time.

Turns out when we're willing to get into the trenches with people and enter into their circumstances, even if we aren't the best equipped, God takes us up on the offer. I assume He has people throughout the world who need cared for and not enough people willing to provide care. At a minimum it's a love-economic problem.

"Jesus went through all the towns and villages, teaching in their synagogues, proclaiming the good news of the kingdom and healing every disease and sickness. When he saw the crowds, he had compassion on them, because they were harassed and helpless, like sheep without a shepherd. Then he said to his disciples, "The harvest is plentiful but the workers are few. Ask the Lord of the harvest, therefore, to send out workers into his harvest field." Matthew 9:35-38

The harvest is plentiful but the workers are few. I love the last verse when Jesus says to ask the Father to send out workers. He knew our efforts wouldn't be enough. We need to pray He helps not only us be courageous and willing, but other workers as well. There is enough work to go around.

Sometimes I think our work will be done. But with God there is always more to do so He asks, we say *yes*, and the journey continues.

16

—

SHELTER OF THE
MOST HIGH

One of the many valuable things a home provides is shelter.

Scripture explains how it's possible to make our dwelling and shelter in God, and that He can protect us and give us rest. Which I love, because it means that because of Jesus, true homelessness, technically, is impossible.

Psalm 91 shows the benefits of acknowledging heaven as home, and God as shelter.

"He had His dwelling
in the Most High.
Whoever dwells in the shelter
of the Most High
will rest in the shadow
of the Almighty."
Psalm 91:1

The Father provides *true* home, shelter, and rest.

So for our friends who don't have a safe physical shelter, it's encouraging to remember they have access to a safe spiritual shelter. And that our genuine encouragement can be a form of shelter for them too.

I think God loves it when we make ourselves shelter for each other.

But unfortunately at the tents, we've witnessed the opposite. Small groups within the tent city have started turning against one another. Some have had their tents vandalized or thrown into the river, and others have had what little they own stolen. Some have even returned to find their tents on fire.

It's hard to believe anyone could harm the helpless, especially when knowing exactly what it feels like to be helpless themselves.

But it's easy to believe that anyone without rest, especially without *rest in the shadow of the Almighty*, is suffering. And suffering can produce some scary things; in this case resentment, paranoia, and anger.

So, down by the tents the suffering has produced more suffering. And people without shelter have turned against people without shelter.

I knew some people were now afraid to go to sleep at night in fear of a disaster. But in God's mercy, He already had a verse prepared to comfort them.

> *If you say, "The Lord is my refuge,"*
> *and you make the Most High your dwelling,*
> *no harm will overtake you,*
> *no disaster will come near your tent.*
> *Psalm 91:9-10*

It literally says *tent!* There is no shelter safer than the *shelter of the Most High*. Even when we are outside sleeping in the cold and dark, afraid of our enemies, God is our safety from disaster.

Even when the only thing between our enemies and us is the thin wall of a tent, there is nothing to fear. Our faith in the Almighty ensures no disaster will come near our tent.

The assurance for us all is that true safety can only be found in the *shelter of the Most High.*

17

—

AVATAR

The girl who taught me the truth about the sign is married, and her husband has an all-consuming dependency on heroin. The more I learn about heroin, the more I realize that all-consuming is the only kind of dependency possible on it. For a while she resisted, but eventually it pulled her in alongside her husband.

This young married couple is the same age we are, but lives a completely different life. Every day they wake up, find something to eat, and then enter a fantasy world. And then they stay in the fantasy world as long as possible.

The way they describe drugs reminds me of the movie Avatar. They have become so attached to a fantasy life that 'coming back' pales in comparison, until living in the real world feels impossible and has nothing left to offer them. They'd rather destroy their bodies and maybe even their lives than face a day here instead of there.

The real trap of Avatar is comparison, and comparison is the thief of joy.

Comparison is tricky. It starts by whispering we should reach for more, for what we think we need or hope we deserve, but then it never stops.

Sometimes we go to lunch with this couple, but usually are asked to drive them to a methadone clinic so they won't get sick when not using. The request for a ride is almost always last minute and when we are already on our way somewhere else. But these rides are by far the best chance we get to connect with this couple.

The more we get to know them the more I see their limitless potential and possibilities in this world. But they don't want this world anymore; they want Avatar. And it seems like once you become a citizen of Avatar you can't make this world your home the same way again.

Maybe you could, but your heart would have to want to. Your desire would have to somehow become sacrificing the life you think you need for the life you've already been given. Comparison would have to die for you to live.

When accepting God's way, we have no choice but to sacrifice the 'better' life we think we need or want, and to choose the future of His design that He's waiting to give us.

> *"Delight yourself in the Lord*
> *and He will give you the*
> *desires of your heart."*
> *Psalm 37:4 (ESV)*

When I was younger I heard this verse and thought it was a way to get what I wanted. But now I see the real offer is for God to shape the desires of my heart to match His own desires. Probably because He knows if I don't surrender in this way I'll try to reach for a thousand other things. And while those things may seem good, they may not be good for me.

He wants to protect us from ourselves. He wants to protect us from the trap of comparison. He wants to protect us from Avatar.

Since He's the designer, it makes sense that only He would fully understand the creations He's made, and what will give them full lives. And it also makes sense that only He is able to create those lives, since only He holds the complete blueprints to it all.

"Now to him who is able to do immeasurably more than all we ask or imagine, according to his power that is at work within us."
Ephesians 3:20

His plans for us are perfect. They are better than anything we could ask for or imagine. They are better than Avatar.

18

—

CELEBRATE

When people celebrate, it's common to toast a sparkling flute of champagne. Or to enjoy a glass of wine, or maybe something a little stronger. But I've seen many of my homeless friends have problems with alcohol and the trap it becomes. It promises to help them escape or forget or take a break. Then it steals more than it gives every single time.

So I have been challenged to consider the way I celebrate.

If a friend has a dependency, the Bible says not to cause them to experience temptation by drinking in front of them (Romans 14). But the problem is, it's hard to know who has a dependency. Likely some just don't call it what it is. Or they can't lay it down even if they feel God might be asking them to.

I would know because I was one of those people.

It seemed acceptable to hang onto this one pleasure and luxury. But of course, acceptable to God and acceptable to me were not the same thing.

So the excuses started. It's not like I had a problem. I wasn't getting drunk which is what the Bible says not to do. I work hard and deserve a break now and then. *I had more excuses than drinks.*

The truth is I knew God didn't want a drop of alcohol in my life anymore. And the reason I knew it was wrong for me is because I could sense it in my spirit every, single, time.

I wish I had an inspiring story to tell about how Jesus asked me to stop drinking and I immediately said yes. But unfortunately that's not what happened. Instead, I just kept having a conversation with my excuses and not with Him.

Anyone who's ever had an idol knows, that the thing you're after isn't even as much of a problem as the heart issues it produces. An inch of us that's holding onto something else is an inch God can't enter into. It becomes hard to receive from Him when our hands are already full clenching something else.

Turns out I did have a problem. It was called entitlement. I wasn't willing to give up a glass of wine with my girlfriends, a beer at a baseball game, a group champagne cheers at celebrations, or a mojito on a hot day. I had associated alcohol with aspects of life, when the truth was, with it I wasn't truly living.

The entitlement was toxic. Anytime I feel I deserve something other than God's love I know I am in trouble.

In fact, the fear alone that I couldn't break free made it an issue. I feared I'd become legalistic or not enjoy life without it, or fear I'd discover through trying to give it up that I couldn't, or wouldn't. So I ignored God about it. Even though I knew by now from experience this never works.

Turns out I wasn't just holding onto it. It was holding onto me too.

The day I tried to give it up, once and for all, was the day I realized how spiritual the hold was. And how the enemy had probably delighted in keeping me distracted, confused, and with divided loyalties for a long time. I decided to put a stake in the ground and prayed for God to take this trap out of my life. As I did this I physically opened up my hands to Him as an act of surrender, and rejected the idol in my heart. That was when I entered the real hurricane.

You don't know how hard the wind is blowing until you turn and walk against it.

This thing I thought was 'not a problem' was holding me hostage in the territory of the enemy. And he didn't want to lose this fight. I became flooded with a cloud of angst, confusion, back-and-forth emotions, and honestly the thought crossed my mind a few times that something wanted to kill me. As crazy as it may sound, I really was experiencing two forces with opposing motives trying to claim me, and I think we all know who those two forces were.

But thankfully, God wins.

After this bizarre battle I fell asleep from complete exhaustion. Then I woke the next morning, and felt free and safe again. Whatever had its hold on me was gone. And I never drank a drop of alcohol again after that, and what's more incredible is that I never even wanted to. God really can break us out of the prisons we create.

"He brought them out of darkness, the utter darkness, and broke away their chains."
Psalm 107:14

Now I have such Good News to share with friends who have some type of dependency or thing they *can't live without.* I own the evidence of a personal testimony that it's a spiritual bond, which *can* be broken, and that freedom is possible. With God all things are possible.

"The Spirit of the Lord is upon me,
for he has anointed me to bring Good News to the poor.
He has sent me to proclaim that captives will be released,
that the blind will see, that the oppressed will be set free."
Luke 4:18 (NLT)

I've seen and I've tasted that God's way of celebrating is better. It's not a drink, it's a state of heart. And it's lasting, and pure, and full of life.

Now that's something to *celebrate*.

19

—

DINNER PARTY

A former homeless man, the one who took us to the tents the very first time, has since become a dear friend of our family. Recently we found out his birthday was approaching and he was without people or plans to celebrate.

We invited him to choose any friend he wanted and come over to our place for dinner. Delighted, he arrived on his birthday with his best friend who we knew well, that lived in a shelter nearby. I was delighted too, because I had recently found a better way of celebrating and couldn't wait to share it with them. No temptations or drama, just food and fun and the best night ever.

When they arrived they were surprised to find our entryway filled with decorations, streamers, and balloons, which were also draped throughout the apartment.

I made the fanciest meal I knew how and we took our time enjoying all the courses. There were appetizers, entrées, and sparkling juice drinks in fancy flutes. The best flatware and silverware we had were brought out for the occasion.

It was probably one of the best dinner parties I'd ever been to because there was zero expectation or pressure. I don't think I'd ever realized until now how much more pressure I felt to perform for my non-homeless friends than my homeless friends. The homeless friends have taught me what freedom in friendship looks like. In the tent community, life is so challenging that no one has the time or energy to worry about superfluous things. It's refreshing.

After dinner we played games, ate cake and ice cream, watched the birthday boy open presents, and laughed when he was afraid to blow out the candles for fear of catching his long beard on fire.

Later that night, after our guests had left and all the cleanup was over, I laid in bed with a huge smile on my face. I just felt so happy. I opened my Bible and miraculously turned right to this verse (Luke 14:12-14), spoken by Jesus:

"When you give a luncheon or dinner,
do not invite your friends, your brothers or relatives,
or your rich neighbors;
if you do, they may invite you back
and so you will be repaid.
But when you give a banquet, invite the poor,
the crippled, the lame, the blind,
and you will be blessed.
Although they cannot repay you,
you will be repaid at the resurrection of the righteous."

Before tonight, I had never thrown a dinner party while needing to be mindful of the time so my guests could get into their shelter lines for admission. I had never offered a fancy meal that even if not fancy, would still have been enjoyed simply because it wasn't shelter food.

But now I can't imagine a better dinner party.

20

—

THE CHANCE

We eventually found out the friend we checked into rehab left after less than a week in the program.

I wouldn't say I was shocked, but definitely disappointed. And upset. And I worried rehab had been the chance for him to finally win his war over drugs.

No one knew where he went after that. People said they saw him here and there but he privately moved to some other place on the streets. I knew he was running; from us, from himself, from what a different life could require, and maybe from God.

Finally he reached out to us and we met at a coffee shop near the tents to catch up. When he arrived I could immediately tell he was back using again.

He said he was sorry. That he couldn't stay in rehab. We said we were disappointed but still here for him, and just wanted him to be free. I was always surprised how God gave me such an unwavering compassion, for him specifically. And I knew it was the mercy of Jesus because even when I was disappointed or angry nothing seemed able to lessen my loyalty. I was grateful to the Holy Spirit for this and also for the chance to clear the air with him.

And then he died.

Less than two weeks later he was found dead outside his tent from a heroin overdose.

In the weeks that followed, I thought of the things I had sincerely appreciated about him. Random things. I loved how we had so frequently visited where one another lived, and how when he chose to be a good leader everyone followed. I loved how when talking with others, he referred to us as his family. I loved how he always complimented my "homemade" blueberry muffins and then talked them up so much around the tents, I didn't have the heart to tell him they came from a box.

But what I loved most was how God used him to change my life and heart. And for that I will always be grateful.

The next time our group visited the tents, we said a prayer for him and shared memories from his life. I passed out his favorite treats that morning and was sad. We went from tent to tent, and it was clear the community was affected by the sudden news. People asked if we knew, and we said yes, and then they asked if we knew how it had happened. We said we didn't really know which was the truth.

In time more potential details surfaced. News travels fast at the tent city, and really, on the streets in general. But no one really knows for sure what happened to him that night, and if it was accidental or intentional. Some said he planned it, but I don't know if that's true. Without identification or record of family, I also heard the city had him cremated almost immediately. But I don't know if that's true either.

There are many things we'll never know. But I know he is without the chance for a life that could have been lived and I am without the chance to say goodbye.

21

—

A SENSE OF HOME

In honor of our friend that died too soon, we went on social media and fundraised to buy heaters, for everyone staying in tents along the river that winter. It would be a tangible way for the warmth of his memory to continue on. And this would be almost exactly a year ago from when we took him the heater, that freezing night in the trenches.

The morning of the heater tent visit I woke up full of anticipation. This had never been done before. All the homeless along the Chicago River had never been given an option for warmth through winter like this before.

We met our group under the bridge that leads to an entrance for the tent city, and it began to snow. We prayed together under the bridge, huddled up with snowflakes slowly falling all around us, and then trekked through winter to the first tent.

The first woman we visited I had never seen before. She was sincerely grateful for the heater, hand warmers, breakfast, and hot coffee. She looked to be newly homeless because there were only a couple of blankets in her tent. We showed her how to safely use the heater, and I gave her my cell number in case she needed anything or wanted to come over sometime.

I asked if she wanted me to pray with her and she said yes.

Then something special happened. Through the Holy Spirit my heart opened, and words filled up my chest and poured out of my mouth for her. It was like God's love was filling up every inch inside her tent. In the stillness of the snow, and the prayer, there was an unmistakable peace meant just for her.

In my experience after the Holy Spirit moves, there is a power and a calm it leaves behind. So she and I sat for a moment in the stillness of the Spirit and the snow. I thought the prayer was for her, but it blessed me, too.

"Praise be to the God and Father
of our Lord Jesus Christ,
the Father of compassion
and the God of all comfort,
who comforts us in all our troubles,
so that we can comfort those in any trouble
with the comfort we ourselves
receive from God."
2 Corinthians 1:3-5

I love coming to the tents but I know it's ultimately God who brings lasting comfort and peace, not us. We hold the hand warmers, blankets, and blueberry muffins, but He holds the promises each heart needs to hear.

We traveled on. A little further down was a large grouping of tents, so we stopped there. Some people we knew and some we didn't. Everyone was so grateful for the heaters, and it seemed this gift brought trust with it, because people opened up to us more than usual about things they were going through.

The heaters brought a sense of relief. The first time a heater was turned on inside their tent, each person would get a new look on their face that said, *"I can do this."*

My prayer was that there would be a person who prayed that morning, *"God please show me you're still here with me"* and then when we arrived unexpectedly with a heater, they would feel their prayer had been answered. That they would know, *God heard me.*

And from what people told us in the months to come after that day, this prayer wasn't just answered for one, but many.

> *"When the righteous cry for help, the Lord hears*
> *and delivers them out of their troubles.*
> *The Lord is near to the brokenhearted*
> *and saves the crushed in spirit.*
> *Many are the afflictions of the righteous,*
> *but the Lord delivers him out of them all."*
> *Psalm 34: 17-19 (ESV)*

God knows what His people need. We've been taking love and food to the tents for over a year. But the heaters that day brought such a different level of support and comfort.

It was like people now felt they could have the chance to experience warmth again, in every way. For the homeless living outside in the winter these heaters have provided a sense of home.

And this experience and these people have provided a sense of home for me too. Because I know that no matter where I live, my home is with people who don't have homes.

22

—

INCONVENIENT LOVE

Sometimes love is inconvenient.

My husband and I had a special date night planned, the night before I was scheduled to travel. The trip had been planned for quite a while, and so had the date.

Before dinner we made a quick stop by the store to pickup some last minute essentials I needed for my trip.

After finding everything we needed, we started heading to the checkout and a man approached us.

He said he was homeless and needed our help. Since we had become involved in the tent community, it was as if we started magically attracting the homeless. Everywhere we went, including people who didn't even know us.

Of all the people in the store that evening, this man had walked directly up to *us*. He asked if he could borrow our cell phone to make a call. Easy *yes*.

He called. No one answered.

Next, he asked if we knew of a place he could stay for the night. That's when this encounter turned potentially inconvenient.

We had a choice to make and could do one of two things at this point.

Option one would be to tell him about the only emergency overnight shelter in the city that would accept him this late in the evening. We could explain how to get there, even Google the address for him so he could see it on our phone, and sincerely wish him the best.

Option two would be to help him find a meal, a bed, and maybe even physically walk him to where he needed to go. This option would almost surely mean canceling our cherished date plans because there would not be time to accomplish both.

We were probably the only people in this store that knew of every homeless shelter option in the city, and the admission timing and requirements for each. So was it a coincidence that he had somehow come directly right up to us?

Our date night turned into taking him to a warm meal and bed for the night.

Of course, abandoning our plans and not being able to connect one-on-one with my husband before the trip disappointed me. But I was pleased by how small and fleeting that disappointment was compared to the excitement of being able to love someone together who needed it.

It unified us together with a sense of purpose and mission that was somehow still romantic. And what really made my heart leap was when I realized that this wasn't a big deal for us anymore. Being inconvenienced for others had become more and more normalized in our marriage, and *that* was a big deal.

It was a milestone in living the way we wanted to live as a family.

"You love as well as you are willing
to be inconvenienced."

Ann Voskamp

Option one would have been the easiest and most 'normal,' but option two required something of us. And only when we stepped into his situation was he relieved of some of his burden, because we were willing to help carry it with him.

When he got a meal it was clear he was starving. He shoveled food in his mouth so fast I thought he might choke. No one talked as he took time to regain energy and gather himself. After a lot of food and a little caffeine, he started coming to life like a completely different person.

As we walked to the shelter he told us a bit of his story. He'd been living homeless on the streets of Chicago for about a week, having just come from Detroit with what sounded like only the clothes he was wearing. We didn't get the whole story and didn't ask.

He got all checked into the shelter safe-and-sound, and when we left he was already introducing himself to people and trying to 'bum a smoke.' I was happy he was safe, not hungry, and not alone.

Walking back home that night we were fulfilled and alive. And we definitely didn't miss the original 'great date' we had planned. What God had planned was so much greater.

Inconvenient love is starting to become my favorite kind.

23

—

PERFECT TIMING

I don't cook often. Lately, summer nights of this young marriage had included ordering in, or picking something up together on our way home. With the ministry work of Luminate being especially demanding in this season, I admittedly hadn't made meal planning a focus. But the good news is, God doesn't rely on my strengths to meet the needs of His people.

Recently, I prepared dinner and made much more than what was needed for the two of us. After we ate there was still plenty leftover.

As I got up from the table, a text came through from our friends at the tents. Their government money had run out for the month and they asked if we had anything to eat.

This was the first time this particular couple had asked for food.

And this was also the first time in recent memory I had made this much food. In God's economy, there is always supply to meet demand.

*"And God will generously provide all you need.
Then you will always have everything you need
and plenty left over to share with others."
2 Corinthians 9:8 (NLT)*

I created some impromptu care packages we could take out to the tents, including the meals, some desserts, and a few other toiletry items we had on hand. I remember standing in our kitchen assembling it all, and how full my heart felt. It was becoming so gratifying to love.

A few weeks later it happened again.

I had carefully prepared a large meal since I was in the mood to bake. It wasn't long before I realized what (or Who) had prompted this mood, because while the food was still hot someone living outside reached out to us for a meal!

Even though cooking has been rare in our home for this season, I have never been without something to give when it is asked of me. God provides every time.

The group that had reached out this most recent time hadn't eaten all day. They were so hungry and appreciative. And I was just as sad to see them desperate as I was relieved by the timing again. Incredible.

The next time it happened was for the woman I had prayed with the morning of the heater visit. She hadn't asked for anything since that prayer, and I not only loved that we could reconnect, but in this way that showed God could and would continue to provide for her when she asked.

It kept happening: a Sunday afternoon after we had just gone grocery shopping, a Wednesday evening when I happened to bake a casserole, and other random times. Perfect times.

"Is anything too hard for the Lord?"
Genesis 18:14

And then recently, there was a provision I saw as nothing short of remarkable.

Following a week of travel, we didn't have much if any food in the house when we returned home. I quickly made a large batch of pasta tossed with parmesan and olive oil. During dishes, we got a text from a married couple asking if we had anything to eat.

Guess what we had left in the house at that time? Two plates leftover from the pasta I had just made, two personal-sized packages of protein trail mix in the cabinet, and two pieces of fruit. If that wasn't enough weird coincidences of two, I'll let you guess how many refreshing cans of sparkling water on that hot summer night were left in the fridge. *Two.*

That hasn't happened before or since, and I know only because it was needed did it happen at all.

I couldn't have anticipated or been prepared for this string of events or needs, and through it was reminded how tangibly God loves us.

I wonder if I was blessed as much as the meal recipients through all of this, because I got to see God provide first-hand in perfect ways. I wonder if this is how the disciples felt, watching Jesus feed five thousand people with five loaves and two fish (Mark 6). It wasn't just the people being fed who were blessed, but the disciples who grew in faith, watching Jesus provide before their eyes.

I shared these mealtime miracles with my unexpected dinner guests so they would know how loved they were, and that their Creator was working things together for them.

> *"And we know that in all things*
> *God works for the good of those who love him,*
> *who have been called according to his purpose."*
> *Romans 8:28*

He loves us so much He prepares us dinner.

The simple truth is: He looks after me, He looks after you, He's in the details, and His timing is always *perfect.*

24

—

DECK OF CARDS

I used to think the hardest part about being homeless was not having a home. My assumption was that the worst part of it all had to be sleeping outside, and that once someone simply gained access to a place to live, it would help them 'get back on their feet' again.

I have since learned the hardest part about homelessness isn't being without a home. I don't even think it's sleeping outside. It's that once you're homeless, the deck to get back out again isn't usually stacked in your favor. That's why temporary homelessness can often turn into a much more permanent sense of hopelessness.

I've seen few things have the ability to transform someone's life the way immersing ourselves into their situation can. But this immersion is costly, and has a way of quickly leading you into a surprisingly complex and complicated web.

Unfortunately homelessness doesn't seem to be as simple as the lack of a home or job; there are a whole host of other issues that are even more difficult to resolve (lack of hope, a self-defeating mindset, destructive behaviors and dependencies, an emotionally or physically paralyzing trauma, unaddressed or undiagnosed illnesses, etc).

My assumptions were changed, and it all started when a homeless friend reached out and asked something she never had before:

"Do you want to grab coffee?"

My mind raced with all the things I needed to do that day. I thought about everything I had planned to accomplish, and the errands I'd been putting off all week that *had* to get done today.

But she had never reached out to me before, and I wondered if she needed to talk about something important. I forced myself to quiet the thoughts in my mind again, take a deep breath, and sit still with God for a minute. Turns out my errands were not as important to Him as the daughter who had just reached out.

I responded to her that yes, I could meet.

Thank God (literally) that when we slow down and pay attention, our own needs and schedules aren't the only factors considered in how we should spend our time. Since He *is* love, when we ask His advice, love becomes the truer, clearer filter through which we can see our lives.

"Do nothing out of selfish ambition or vain conceit.
Rather, in humility value others above yourselves,
not looking to your own interests
but each of you to the interests of the others."
Philippians 2:3-4

This girl needed more than a cup of coffee. She was in a crisis. She explained how her husband was mentally ill and needed to pick-up his monthly medication from the State. But the medication had been less important than more pressing needs over the past two months, and the lack of chemical consistency was starting to show itself in alarming ways.

For example, she wasn't allowed to communicate with anyone but him. She also wasn't allowed to step outside the tent without his permission.

She didn't know what to do, and had basically contacted me out of desperation.

We ordered coffee drinks, a few pastries, and sat down. After talking for a while several issues came to the surface. It was clear they needed to find housing, that she had a deep desire to regain custody of her children, and that her husband needed his medication. I asked, of all three issues, which one did she think was most important for us to address first? She immediately replied, *"the third one."*

So we spent the day tackling #3.

I thought this would obviously be the easiest to accomplish of the three, and would simply involve me driving to a pharmacy and providing them with the necessary prescription money. Nope.

This coffee date turned into a seven-hour day that gave me a window into the complexities of homelessness.

The medication was through the State, which meant there was only one hospital that could give us what we needed. After we drove through traffic to an overcrowded Medical Center, we waited in line for an hour. I assumed what we were waiting in line for was the prescription. Wrong again. What we were waiting in line for was the opportunity to talk with someone, who could pass us on to another room filled with more people in chairs. Then we waited in that next room for another hour.

As we sat there and I felt my productive day slipping away, it was hard not to get impatient. But I considered how difficult today would have been for this couple to accomplish on their own. Parking was $10 and bus fare would have been about the same. There were no shelters in this part of the city so unless they ate at a restaurant, which would have cost even more than the prescription, they would also have had to go all day without eating.

Finally, we were called. A woman from the Medical Center told us that in order to receive free prescription fills through the State, we needed a letter. When we said we didn't have a letter, she said it "would have been mailed to the place of residence." My friends then had no choice but to explain to her, in front of the line of people standing behind us, that their residence was a tent located in a deserted railroad site. They couldn't receive mail. The woman seemed unsympathetic, but waved us through to the next waiting area.

The deck didn't seem stacked our favor. So we waited.

> *"And now, Lord, for what do I wait?*
> *My hope is in You."*
> *Psalm 39:7 (NASB)*

Eventually the doctor approved the prescription to be filled, which we were told would take three to four hours, based on their high volume of demand. I needed some fresh air and suggested that while we wait, we grab lunch and visit shelters to check for openings.

Lunch was a welcomed break for all of us. Afterward, we visited three shelters that all had waiting lists several months out, were completely full, or had programs we didn't qualify for (all male/female shelters don't accept married couples).

The day was exhausting in every way. But I was still holding it together until we returned for the prescription. As we got to the pickup window the doctor asked for my friend's ID.

I watched as she reached into her bag and pulled out, no joke, a deck of cards. She silently grabbed the top 'card' off the deck from inside the box: her driver's license.

It was then and there that hot tears started to well up in my eyes. Because I saw the deck of cards for what it was. As if everything she was faced with wasn't enough, she had to hide her ID in a place of seeming little value in case she got jumped. Yet another reality of the streets.

The doctor reviewed the ID and give it back to my friend, who quickly placed it back into the deck.

Speechless.

This experience is etched in my mind, as a painful reminder of the many layers of homelessness. There are so many more things to fight and fear when homeless than sleeping outside. Maybe even more than 52.

25

—

GENEROSITY OPPORTUNITY

Believe it or not I can't remember a single time any of our homeless friends have asked us for money. They've asked us to drive them places, or help them apply for things, or for meals or showers. But never money.

Except just once. A friend in our community, an older man who actually used to be homeless and no longer was, ran into a series of financial issues and asked if we could help him out. Normally, we would have said yes. But living in Chicago was expensive and we were at capacity in our budget for the month. This would be the expense to put us in a tight spot.

So my husband and I discussed, and decided to move things around to help out. We made arrangements to leave work early and meet up with him at the bank to draw cash.

Little did we know, that afternoon would be the last time we'd ever see him again. The next morning he was hit by a train and killed.

My memory of the last time we saw him is treasured now. It made our friendship deeper to enter a tough spot in life together.

We had given him a hug, the envelope, and then stayed to catch up for a while. Turns out, at the time, none of us really knew what was inside the envelope. My husband and I somehow miscommunicated about the amount, and had included twice what he asked for. Later we just assumed that must have been the amount God wanted him to have.

As we were all turning to part ways on the busy street corner downtown, I yelled past all of the people to him with an inside and sarcastic joke, which I knew was his favorite. He laughed a belly laugh that, for a moment, pulled back the veil of his trial and showed us his spirit. That face, in mid-laughter, is now what I remember most when I think of him.

What a thoughtful gift from a thoughtful Father to give us that bright last memory together, when only He knew what would happen the very next day.

Many friends coordinated a celebration of his memory. There was a guestbook in which people wrote sincere notes to the family, and a lot of food to warm our bellies and provide comfort. We had a worship session together of just a few string instruments and voices, and he would have loved it. It was simple and genuine just like he was. After the food was gone and the songs were over, people still stayed for hours, sitting and sharing the nuisances and characteristics that were uniquely his. One was his sense of humor.

I'm grateful we saw him one last time and that what I remember most about him is his laugh. I'm also grateful we didn't turn away from this opportunity to be generous because I would have regretted that the rest of my life.

Who knows what impact generosity really has or if we'll ever know, but this was a lesson learned for us to take every chance we get to engage in generosity, and with gratitude.

26

—

MOVING FORWARD

That coming year, I would receive a gift that was unexpected and not even something I told anyone I wanted. And I have no idea how but it arrived just in time for my birthday.

Everyone knows helping a friend move is a big undertaking. Being asked to help a friend move on a Saturday is even worse. So I'm definitely surprised to say that my incredible birthday gift turned out to be my friends asking me to help them move – on a Saturday.

But things are different now because I have friends who are homeless. And when a homeless friend asks you to help them move, it's a completely different experience.

After years of homelessness, a family close to us was ready to move from their tent and into a home. They were finally able to leave the cardboard, shopping carts, and garbage behind. It was pure exhilaration to pack their stuff into our car and drive away together, literally leaving homelessness in the rear view mirror.

I've heard of people 'getting off the streets' before but had never seen it actually happen. Picking someone up (especially someone you care about) from a tent in the middle of winter, and driving them to their new warm home, felt like a once in a lifetime experience.

But I hope it isn't once in a lifetime. As we drove into their new chapter of freedom, and I saw that it was possible, I was inspired to be a part of this process for as many people as possible.

It was hard to believe how so many years of captivity were brought to an end with just a twenty-minute drive. A different kind of life for this family had felt so far away, so unattainable, and so much further than twenty minutes.

We shared their excitement, but mostly their relief from the weight we'd seen them carry.

No more sleeping outside, no more freezing nights, no more weeks without showers or clean clothes, no more difficulties finding or cooking food. And most importantly, no more hopelessness in assuming this is how it was always going to be.

I didn't think any birthday could ever mean more than the original birthday I spent with the homeless that very first time. But part of that experience had still been about me, and this was completely about them. Last time I had been the one who felt liberated, but this time they experienced liberation. Last time I was celebrated, and this time I celebrated them.

And what better celebration is there than seeing someone you love move forward.

27

—

DIFFERENT KIND OF MINISTRY

The newly free family hosted a housewarming party. At their new home.

We walked down their street and up to their front doorstep, not their tent, to be invited in. Now they were hosting *us*. Now they were serving *us*. Now none of us were homeless anymore, just friends who all want to move forward in life.

Saying the usual housewarming party guest script of "we're so happy for you" didn't seem to quite capture the relief, thanksgiving and joy I felt. Although I didn't know what to say when we arrived, and in the moment found myself saying just that. But I really meant it.

We celebrated with dinner, gifts, and cake. All just icing on top of the sweetness of stability.

One first step toward stability can be enough to show someone an entire staircase of possibility that was once invisible. And not just for other people, but for them.

Sometimes we still take our no-longer-homeless friends breakfast and hot coffee. Not because they need it anymore, but because it's still fun.

Whether I'm spending time with my homeless or non-homeless friends, I've realized the best ministry I can offer is friendship. Not handouts, or food, or even opportunities, but a piece of myself. A willingness to interrupt my life and enter into theirs.

> *"Greater love has no one than this,*
> *that someone lay down his life*
> *for his friends."*
> *John 15:13 (ESV)*

A different kind of ministry could eliminate the need for itself if we personally entered people's lives to help them identify and take their next step forward. A focus not on pity but progress: making homelessness a thing of their past.

I'm all for loving this tent community that has formed. But over the course of the past several months, we've seen almost half of the homeless transition from tents to housing. In fact, much of the land within tent city has become empty as groupings of people move to more stable situations. Slowly it's become evident that things are changing, which seems to inspire those remaining to leave as well. I can't help but think God doesn't just want us to love our neighbors, but to love them as we would want to be loved if in their situation – out of homelessness.

"Love your neighbor as yourself."
Mark 12:31

After being involved with the homeless as we have, I know without a shadow of a doubt that if I were homeless, I wouldn't want to be homeless anymore. Which means if someone were to really love me, they would try to help me get out of that situation. They would care about what I care about. They would know I don't just want compassion or food, but someone to care enough about me and to believe enough in me, to help me get unstuck and back into a place in life where I could thrive again.

Loving people, one-by-one, out of the cycle they're in until there was no longer a need for the ministry, would be the best ministry I can think of. The great part is this doesn't require a program or nonprofit, just people around us. And we all have that.

Lately this ministry for us has become a goal of identifying someone who wants to get out of homelessness, and is ready to do what it takes to help make that a reality, and literally saying *out loud* to them: *"You're Next."*

You're next to get out of here. You're next to climb up out of this tent and into your future. And we will help you do whatever it takes to get there.

In Christ, there is always a next step forward. There is always a "glory to glory" potential ahead (2 Corinthians 3:18). Maybe ministry is just being friends with someone and saying "I'm going to move forward in your next step with you."

They can tell if you mean it, and if you're already friends they might even believe you. That seems like real ministry to me.

I want my focus to be a lifestyle of friendship through Christ that can move forward those around me. I want my focus to be a different kind of ministry.

28

—

GRATEFUL GOODBYES

When I arrived in Chicago ten years ago I had so much to learn. And even though that's still true, I now feel responsible to a city I've learned so much in and grown so much from.

After a series of open doors and confirmations the previous spring, it became clear to our family that God was preparing the next chapter of life for us in Atlanta, Georgia. So that fall our little family would make a big move six hundred miles south.

God did amazing things during our time in Chicago, and He will do amazing things during our time in Atlanta. Because Amazing is who He is.

Weeks of packing, pizza, and prayer followed. As I processed my time in Chicago, I thought about this epic city where I was saved, married, launched a ministry, and learned to love. A lot had happened in ten years; some good, some bad, but ultimately it was the God-things I remember most and that made the mark on me.

When it was confirmed we were moving, we spread the news. One of my now closest friends (with the deck of cards) offered to co-host a going away party for us. The time we spent shopping and party-prepping together was so inspiring. Even though she didn't have a home to host in, she still wanted to extend a heart of hospitality and help us celebrate our next step forward.

She and I ended up co-throwing the party on a Sunday afternoon at my apartment rooftop. We had about thirty guests. One of our formerly homeless friends who was now a chef, offered to be the grill master and handle the burgers and brats for everyone. My husband bought lots of fantastic food, and we went overboard on the budget on purpose. Everyone had fun and no one left hungry.

I thought it might feel sad, but it actually wasn't sad at all. What it felt like was a celebration of what God had done during this season, the relationships He had built, and the needs He had met for all of us. An altar was built in my heart through the party that afternoon.

Some of our closest friends stayed later. The people we've been visiting and spending time with for years were included in that group, and as I looked around I felt so grateful to be here. I remembered how many of these relationships had started with my birthday that first year, and how far we'd all come since then. The things we'd overcome. Who we had become.

After the party, some asked if they could take my husband and me to lunch or to coffee before the move. Not at a shelter, not at the tents, but out at a restaurant. It was a true gesture of sacrifice to share what little I knew they had.

The beauty of this power paradox is one of the things I've cherished most about our time in Chicago. It's not about how much you have, but how much you are willing to give of yourself and get into the trenches for others. It's powerful, it's a picture of who Jesus is, and it's how we were meant to live.

Throughout this fulfilling, challenging, exhausting and exhilarating time, God was near. In the time I spent here I learned more about God and myself than anywhere else I had lived. I experienced the simple, thin silver lining of life. I had experienced the gospel.

All of us have more moves forward to make in the years ahead, and I don't yet know what this one will bring for us. But I do know that if I hold what I learned in my heart, and always remember these people and places, I can say goodbye with gratitude.

29

—

CITY OF LIGHTS

When Jesus spoke again to the people, he said,
"I am the light of the world.
Whoever follows me will never walk in darkness,
but will have the light of life."
John 8:12

No matter where we live in this world we will always have a neighbor in a literal or figurative sense. There will always be light available for us to reflect, and someone who needs to see it.

We've lived in Atlanta for a year now and have already seen how God used our time in Chicago to teach us to love; anywhere. Everywhere. Our neighbors are not homeless anymore but that doesn't mean they need Jesus any less. Or that we serve them any less. Our home and hearts have now been opened for good.

The concept of home is sometimes thought of as family, warmth, peace, and security. And we can all be those things to someone. So we can all be home to someone. Then no one will be homeless anymore, at least not alone.

I realize now the memory of that first flower gift when I was four years old was important because it was the foreshadowing of what I had to relearn twenty years later. I needed to remember the power of a single act for a single person.

Jesus was the first gift and the true gift in that story. He was the one who prompted me to notice and love my neighbor for the very first time.

For the entire law
is fulfilled in keeping this one command:
"Love your neighbor as yourself."
Galatians 5:14

He delights in orchestrating everything necessary to show us He cares for us when our head is in our hands. Over the years God has brought people to be a light for me or has asked me to do so for others.

Jesus is that light. All we have to do is say yes when He asks us to hand someone a flower. All we have to do is reflect His light to others and together we can create an entire city of lights.

ABOUT THE AUTHOR

Lynne Moyer is the Founder & CEO of Luminate Marketing, an international speaker and an award-winning strategist for churches and nonprofits.

Lynne is passionate about speaking on behalf of those who don't have a voice, leveraging influence with purpose, and living a lifestyle of hospitality.

She and her husband, Matt, live in Atlanta, Georgia.

Find Lynne online at LynneMoyer.com.

SCRIPTURE & QUOTE REFERENCES

"Whoever loves money
never has enough;
whoever loves wealth is never satisfied
with their income.
This too is meaningless."
Ecclesiastes 5:10

Chapter 03 | God of this City | Page 19

"You're the God of this city
You're the King of these people
You're the Lord of this nation

You're the Light in this darkness
You're the Hope
to the hopeless

You're the Peace to the restless
There is no one like our God

For greater things have yet to come
And greater things are still to be done
in this city"
"God of this City" Song Lyrics

"Jesus looked at them and said,
With man this is impossible,
but with God all things are possible."
Matthew 19:26

"Come," he said. Then Peter got down
out of the boat, walked on the water
and came toward Jesus.
But when he saw the wind,
he was afraid and, beginning to sink,
cried out, "Lord, save me!"
Immediately Jesus reached out his hand
and caught him,

"You of little faith,"
he said, "why did you doubt?"
Matthew 14:29-31

"Nothing is more powerful than
an idea whose time has come."
Author Unknown

"Jesus replied, "Foxes have dens and
birds have nests, but the Son of Man
has no place to lay his head."
Luke 9:58

"Carry each other's burdens, and in this
way you will fulfill the law of Christ."
Galatians 6:2

*"For we brought nothing into the world,
and we can take nothing out of it.
But if we have food and clothing,
we will be content with that."*
1 Timothy 6:7-8

*"Then he said to them, "Watch out!
Be on your guard against all kinds of
greed; life does not consist in
an abundance of possessions."*
Luke 12:15

*"Remember those who are in prison,
as though you were in prison with them.
Remember those who are suffering,
as though you were suffering
as they are."*
Hebrews 13:3 (GNT)

Chapter 12 | Getting into the Trenches |
Page 64

*"Compassion or forgiveness shown toward
someone whom it is within one's power to
punish or harm. It is performed out of a
desire to relieve suffering that is
motivated by compassion."*
Definition of Mercy

Chapter 14 | Amazing Mercy | Page 74

*"The free and unmerited favor of God,
as manifested in the salvation of sinners
and the bestowal of blessings.
Or courteous goodwill."*

Definition of Grace

Chapter 14 | Amazing Mercy | Page 74

"Amazing mercy how sweet the sound
That saved a wretch like me.
I once was lost but now I'm found.
Was blind but now I see.
'Twas mercy that taught
my heart to fear
And mercy my fears relieved.
How precious did that mercy appear
The hour I first believed.

Through many dangers, toils and snares,
I have already come;
Tis mercy hath brought me safe thus
far, And mercy will lead me home.
Amazing mercy, how sweet the sound
That saved a wretch like me.

I once was lost, but now I'm found.
Was blind, but now I see."

Amazing Grace lyrics (Mercy inserted)

Chapter 14 | Amazing Mercy | Page 75

"Grace is God giving us what we don't
deserve, and mercy is God not
giving us what we do deserve."
Author Unknown

Chapter 14 | Amazing Mercy | Page 76

"Jesus went through all the towns and
villages, teaching in their synagogues,
proclaiming the good news of the kingdom
and healing every disease and sickness.

When he saw the crowds,
he had compassion on them,
because they were harassed and helpless,
like sheep without a shepherd.
Then he said to his disciples,
"The harvest is plentiful
but the workers are few.

*Ask the Lord of the harvest, therefore,
to send out workers into his harvest field."
Matthew 9:35-38*

Chapter 15 | The Journey Continues |
Page 79

*"He had His dwelling in the Most High.
Whoever dwells in the shelter of the Most
High will rest in the shadow
of the Almighty."
Psalm 91:1*

Chapter 16 | Shelter of the Most High |
Page 82

*"If you say, "The Lord is my refuge,"
and you make the Most High your
dwelling, no harm will overtake you,
no disaster will come near your tent."
Psalm 91:9-10*

Chapter 16 | Shelter of the Most High |
Page 83

*"Delight yourself in the Lord and He will
give you the desires of your heart."*
Psalm 37:4 (ESV)

Chapter 17 | Avatar | Page 87

*"Now to him who is able to do
immeasurably more than all we ask
or imagine, according to his power
that is at work within us."*
Ephesians 3:20

Chapter 17 | Avatar | Page 88

*"He brought them out of darkness,
the utter darkness, and broke
away their chains."*
Psalm 107:14

"The Spirit of the Lord is upon me,
for he has anointed me to bring
Good News to the poor.
He has sent me to proclaim that captives
will be released, that the blind will see,
that the oppressed will be set free."
Luke 4:18 (NLT)

"When you give a luncheon or dinner,
do not invite your friends, your brothers
or relatives, or your rich neighbors;
if you do, they may invite you back and so
you will be repaid. But when you give a
banquet, invite the poor, the crippled, the
lame, the blind, and you will be blessed.
Although they cannot repay you,
you will be repaid at the
resurrection of the righteous."
Luke 14:12-14

Chapter 19 | Dinner Party | Page 97

"Praise be to the God and Father of our Lord Jesus Christ, the Father of compassion and the God of all comfort, who comforts us in all our troubles, so that we can comfort those in any trouble with the comfort we ourselves receive from God."
2 Corinthians 1:3-5

Chapter 21 | Sense of Home | Page 105

"When the righteous cry for help, the Lord hears and delivers them out of their troubles. The Lord is near to the brokenhearted and saves the crushed in spirit. Many are the afflictions of the righteous, but the Lord delivers him out of them all."
Psalm 34: 17-19 (ESV)

*"You love as well as you are willing
to be inconvenienced."*
Ann Voskamp

*"And God will generously provide all you
need. Then you will always have
everything you need and plenty
left over to share with others."*
2 Corinthians 9:8 (NLT)

"Is anything too hard for the Lord?"
Genesis 18:14

"And we know that in all things God works for the good of those who love him, who have been called according to his purpose."
Romans 8:28

"Do nothing out of selfish ambition or vain conceit. Rather, in humility value others above yourselves, not looking to your own interests but each of you to the interests of the others."
Philippians 2:3-4

"And now, Lord, for what do I wait? My hope is in You."
Psalm 39:7 (NASB)

"Greater love has no one than this, that someone lay down his life for his friends."
John 15:13 (ESV)

Chapter 27 | Different Kind of Ministry | Page 138

"Love your neighbor as yourself."
Mark 12:31

Chapter 27 | Different Kind of Ministry | Page 139

"And we all, who with unveiled faces contemplate the Lord's glory, are being transformed into his image with ever-increasing glory, which comes from the Lord, who is the Spirit."
2 Corinthians 3:18

Chapter 27 | Different Kind of Ministry | Page 140

"When Jesus spoke again to the people,
he said, "I am the light of the world.
Whoever follows me will never walk in
darkness, but will have the light of life."
John 8:12

Chapter 29 | City of Lights | Page 147

"For the entire law is fulfilled
in keeping this one command:
"Love your neighbor as yourself."
Galatians 5:14

Chapter 29 | City of Lights | Page 148